YES I HAVE SOFTBALL FEVER

Copyright © 2022 by Yes I Have Anxiety, Inc.

All rights reserved.

Thank you for purchasing an authorized edition of this book and for complying with copyright laws by not reproducing, scanning, or distributing any part of it in any form without permission.

Consumer Use Disclaimer: The "Yes I Have" book series was created in light-hearted, relatable fun to create distractions from things individuals may be dealing with. All "Yes I Have" books are not intended to diagnose medical conditions nor provide a cure for any medical conditions. This book is not meant to be a replacement for real medical intervention if needed.

ISBN: 978-1-958083-10-9

First Edition: April 2022

Yes I Have Anxiety, Inc.
Grove, Ok 74345

WHAT ARE YOU DEALING WITH?
WE GOT YOU!

Visit www.YesIHave.com for more books!

Do you have an idea for the next "Yes I Have®" book? Reach out to us through our website!

You might just see your idea in a future book!

What are you dealing with?

Design a Cool Softball Uniform!

Write Meaningful Notes to Your Teammates all Over This Page.

HOMERUN BALL! Write the Date of the Day you Hit Your First Homerun.

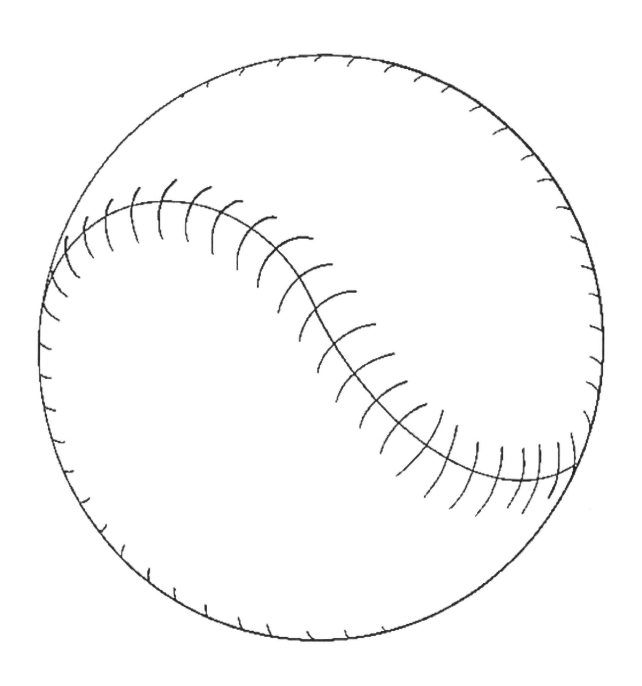

Decorate Your Facemask.

STATE TIME! Make Some State Send Off Posters.

What does Your Championship Trophy Look Like?

Tournament Time! What is on Your Packing List?

_____

_____

_____

_____

_____

_____

_____

_____

_____

_____

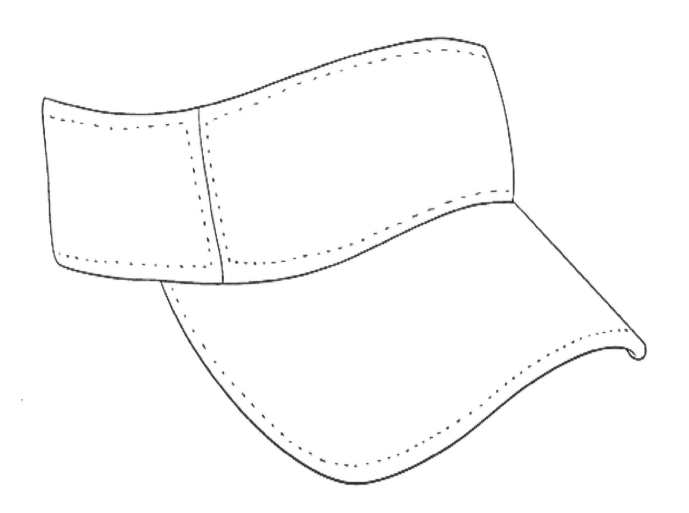

Make Your Visor Stand Out!

What are Your Favorite Team Bonding Activities?

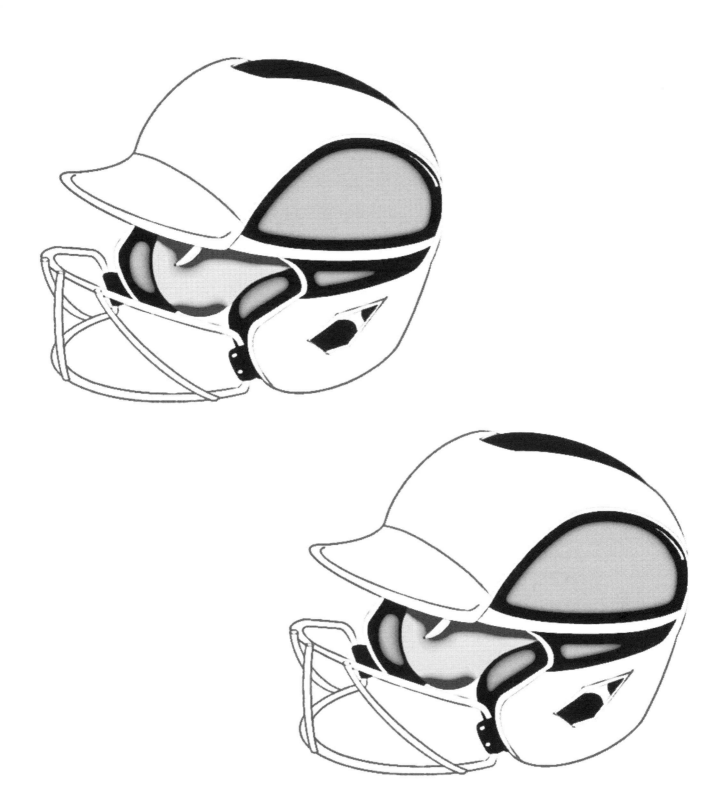

Make a Cool Helmet and Then an Ugly Helmet.

Design Your Championship Ring!

Draw Your Rival Mascot and Then Black it Out.

Put Tags on the Suitcases With Your Favorite Softball Destinations.

Design Your Dream Glove!

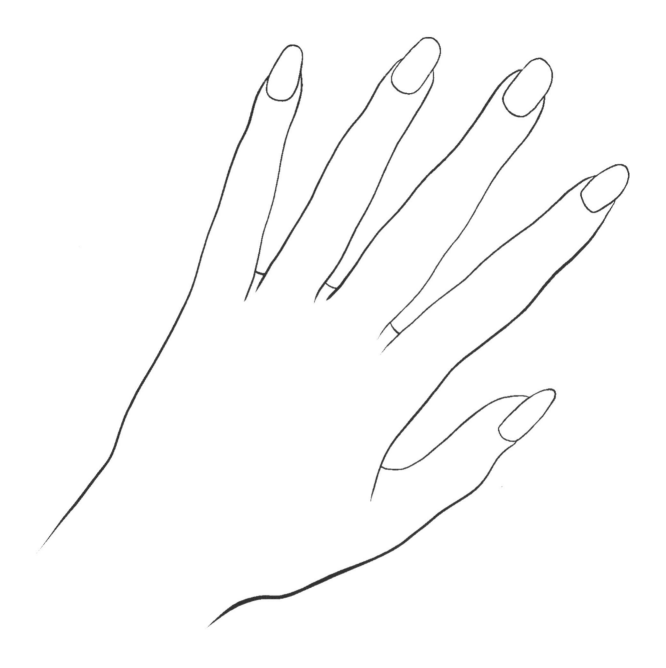

Paint Your Gameday Nails!

Make Your Cleats Super Unique!

Spruce Up Your Headband!

Write Down All of Your Favorite Pre-Game Chants!

Use the Mud from Your Cleats to Paint a Picture on This Page!

How Many Softball Words can you Find?

```
C T R I P L E C A T C H E R N
C G R S T R I K E O U T D R S
Z F R I C S H O R T S T O P E
I N O O G L R U K Y T I U C C
T L F R U H E U E T M U B C O
U H I I C N T A N W U B L L N
N B I N R E D F T D E P E P D
I U A R E S O B I S O W S I B
F N H L D D T U A E H W I T A
O T O P L B R B T L L V N C S
R G M O R S A I A F L D G H E
M L E P A O G S V S M O L E C
T O R F N S X L E E E U E R F
A V U L L E F T F I E L D D V
G E N Y C E N T E R F I E L D
```

Design Your Catcher's Gear.

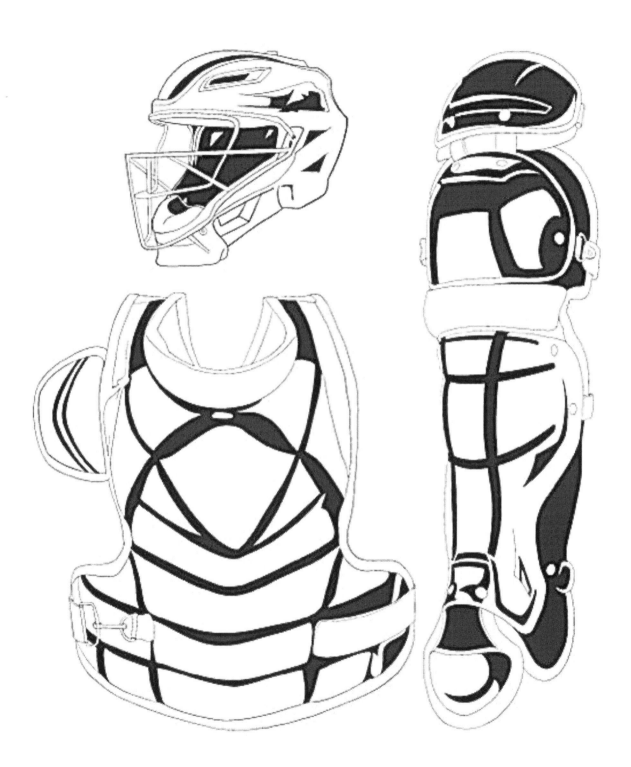

Make This Gum POP!

Glue your Favorite Snack Wrappers to this Page.

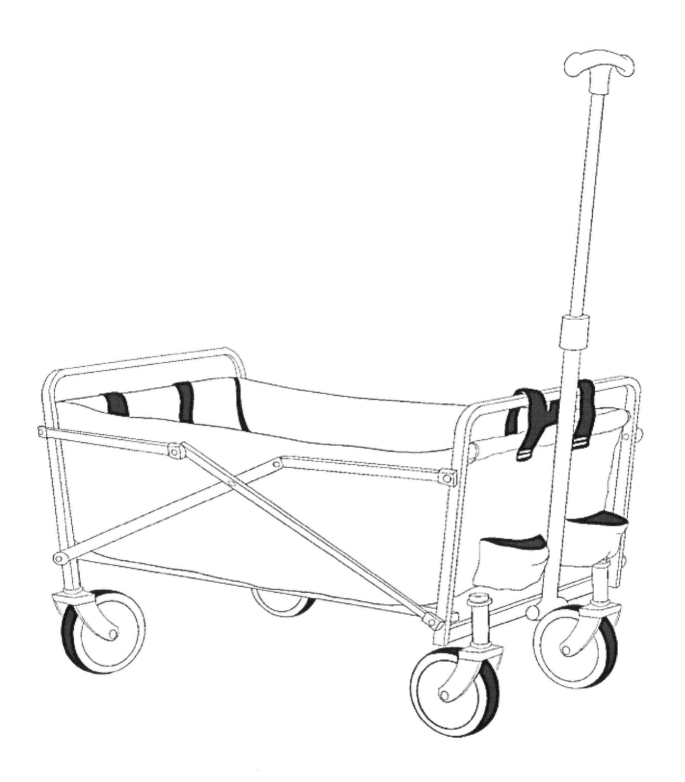

Pimp Out Your Equipment Wagon!

Your Crush is Here! Make the Butterflies Go Away!

Clean Off the Dirt!

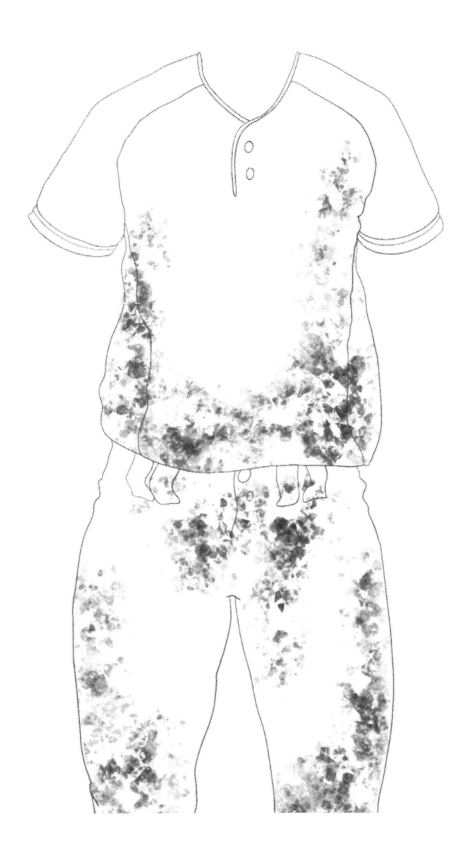

Create Your Own Lineup!

 # TEAM _____

Opponent _____   Location _____   Date _____

Order	NO.	Player	Position	NO.	Substitutes
1					
2					
3					
4					
5					
6					
7					
8					
9					
10					
11					
12					
13					
14					
15					
16					
17					

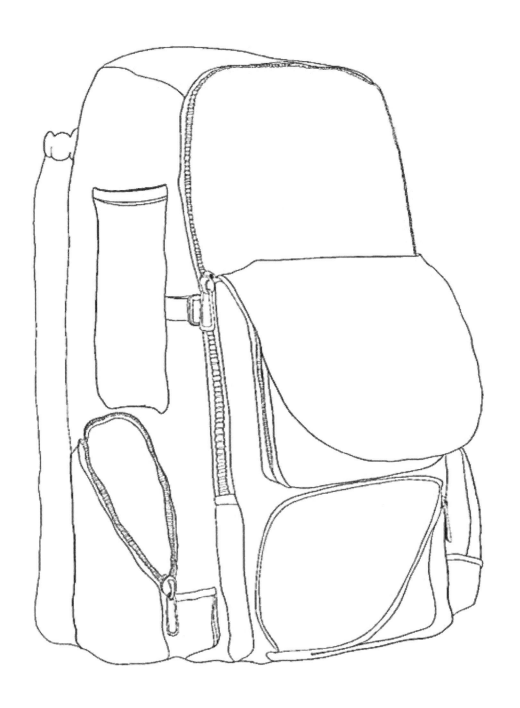

Decorate Your Softball Bag and Fill it With What You Carry.

Decorate Your Hacky Sacks.

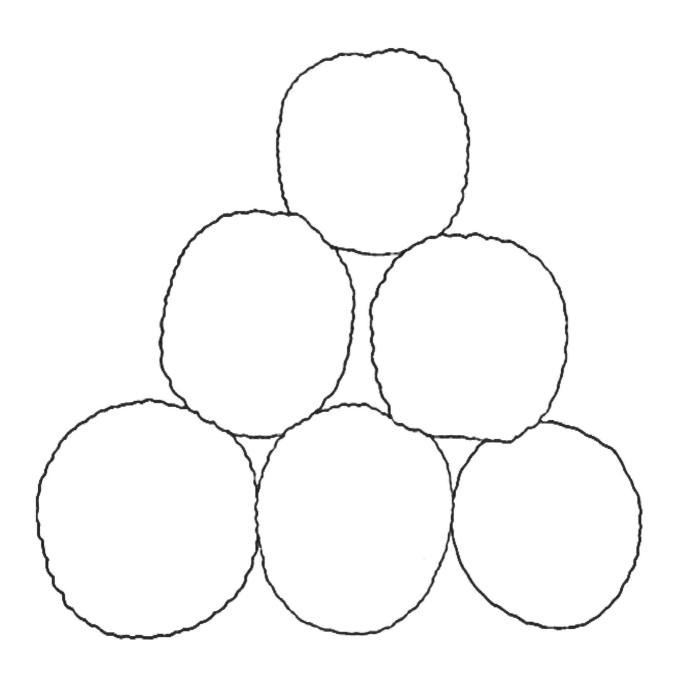

Write Your Favorite Inspirational Quotes All Over This Page.

What Teams Have you Played for or Found Inspiration From to Build Your Foundation?

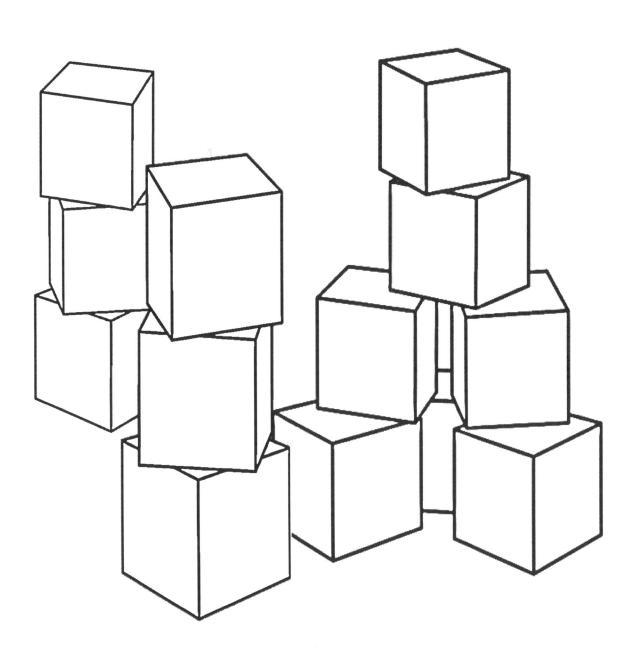

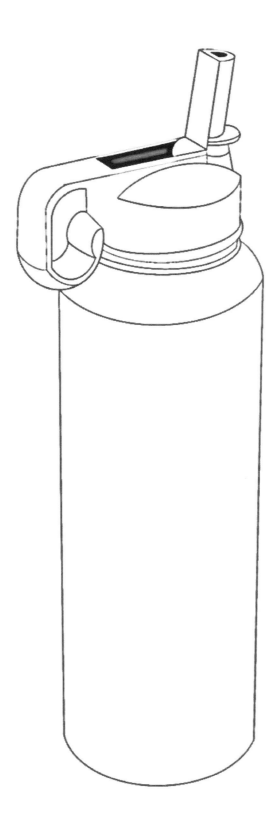

Decorate Your Practice Water Bottle!

Are Rainbow Sunflower Seeds a Thing?

Game Break! Paint Your Favorite Restaurant Logo With a Fork and Spoon.

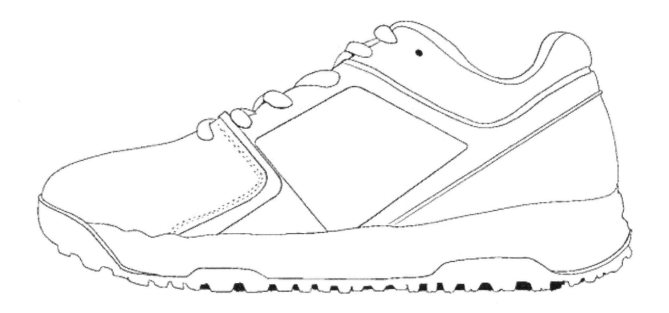

Add Spikes to the Cleats.

What does Your Coach Repeat Too Many Times? Write it All Over the Page.

Give Your Energy Drink Some Energy!

You Sucked Today.
How are you Feeling Emojis?

Write the Lyrics to Your Favorite Warm Up Song!

Bedazzle Your Softball bat.

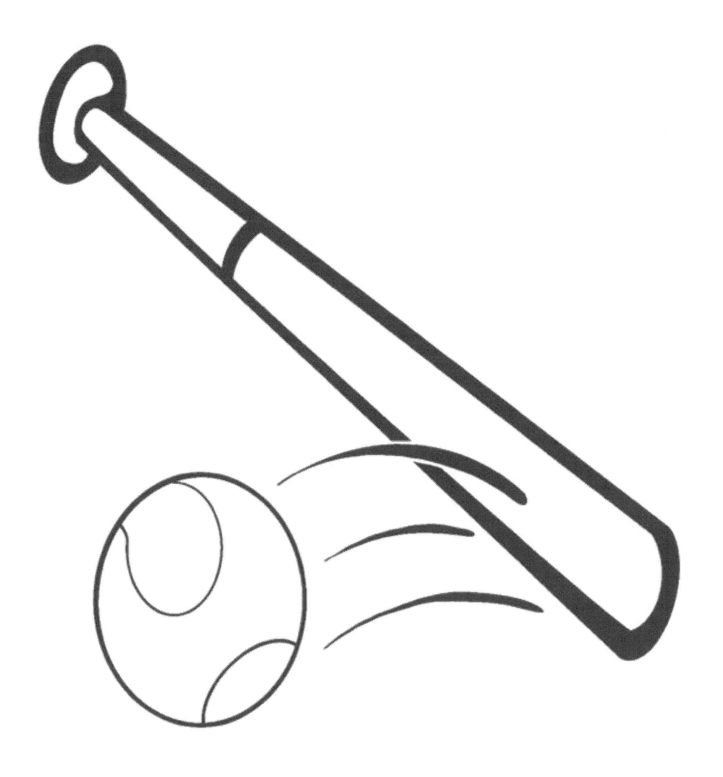

Glue Pictures of Your Favorite Team Memories.

Cover This Entire Page with Real or Fake Popcorn!

Add Some Color to This Field and Make it Come to Life!

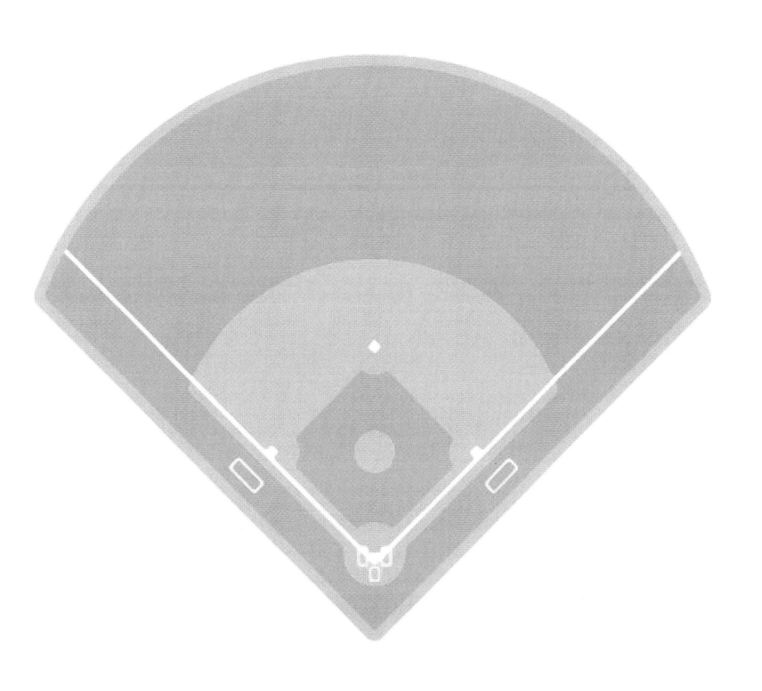

Compare Softball and Baseball!

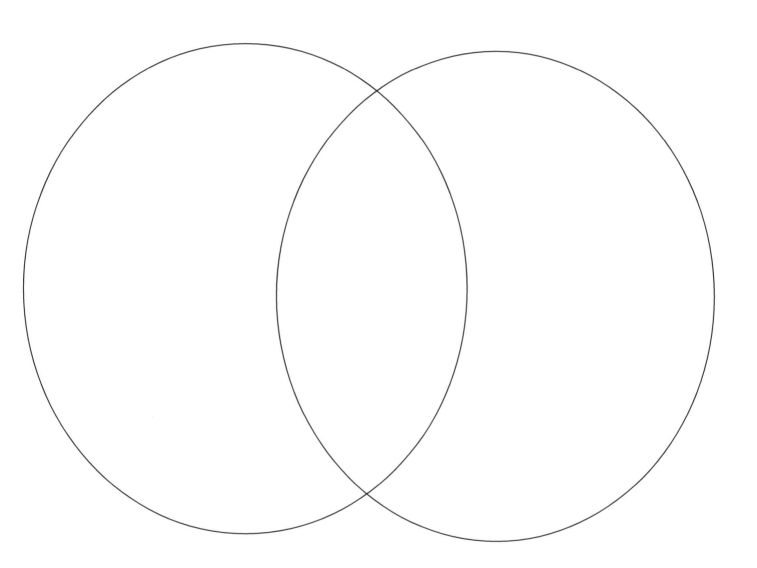

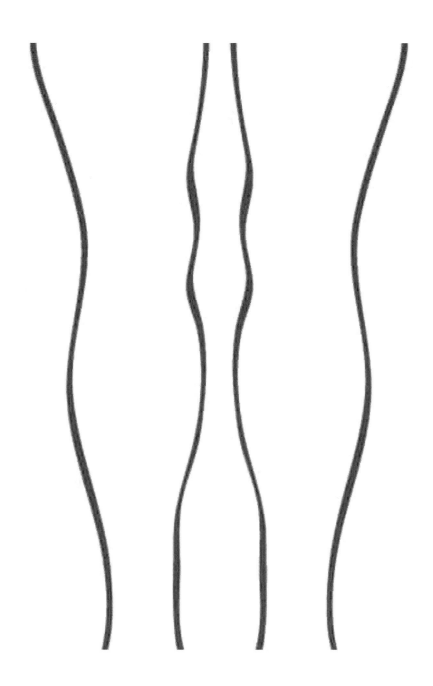

Softballs are NOT Soft. Add Bruises to the Legs.

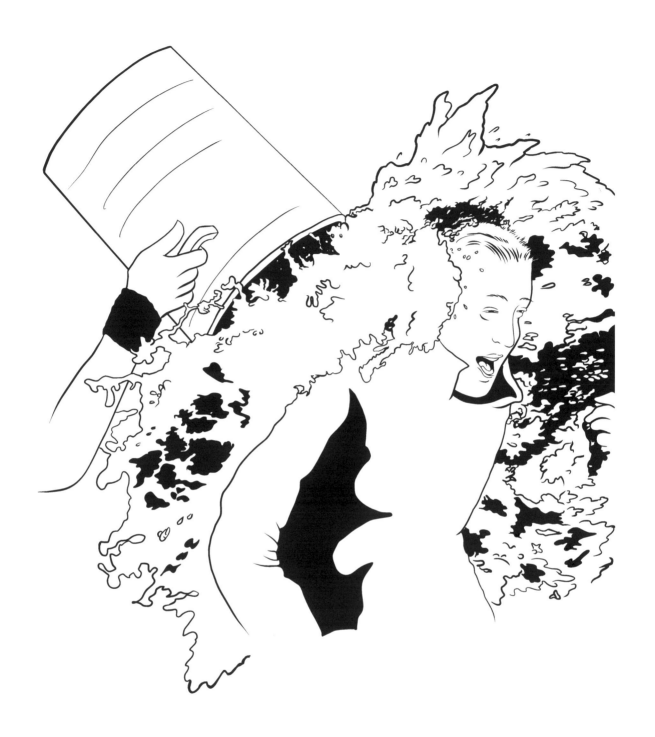

YOU WON STATE! Dump the Jug on Your Coach.

Don't miss out on **FREE books** and New Book Announcements!!!

Follow us on our social media platforms to be included in weekly giveaways, book tour location announcements, new book releases, and videos for page idea inspiration!!!

| officialyesihave | yesihaveofficial | Yes I Have Books | Yes I Have Official |

JOIN OUR NEWSLETTER!:
Text
YESIHAVE
To 22828 to get started!

Hey Fans!! If you post your page videos on social media and one goes viral, we want to know! Send your video to us at yesihavebooks@gmail.com

We showcase our viral fan videos on our website and social media outlets! We have 100+ viral videos and counting!

Want to Find More Books?

Scan the QR Code, Then Decorate it!

Mood Swings Perfectionism
Kids Anxiety Stress Ideas
Hard Times Pets Boredom
Baby Fever Christmas Fever

Made in the USA
Middletown, DE
26 November 2022

16054765R00062